Navigating the Lifecycle of Working Moms in Healthcare

A Working Mom Series

Adrienne J. Towsen, M.D. &
Lisa Piliero Drozdowski, M.S., PA-C

Copyright © 2025 by Working Mom Publishing

All Rights Reserved.

This book or parts thereof may not be reproduced in any form, stored in any retrieval system, or transmitted in any form by any means- electronic, mechanical, photocopy, recording, or otherwise- without prior written permission of the publisher. For permission requests, write to the publisher, "Attention: Permissions Coordinator" at the email address below:

concierge@theworkingmom.us

ISBN: 979-8-218-99899-8

1st Edition

The Working Mom" logo is under active trademark by the U.S. Patent and Trademark Office: Serial Number: 88811251

The Working Mom, LLC
www.TheWorkingMom.us

This book is dedicated to our moms, Rita Towsen & Sandra Piliero, who taught us how to be strong women and how to raise strong women!

Lisa's Story

In the beginning......we were clueless.

I remember the day my daughter Maggie was born. I had a Cesarean section, and when my doctor made the incision to bring her into this world, I asked him if there was a manual that popped out with her. No one can prepare us for the birth of our first child. You will be filled with happiness, shock, and awe. You will get TONS of advice, some wanted, and some unwanted. Take the grains of knowledge you want and toss out the rest! You are now the queen of your universe!

I was raised in Chester County, Pennsylvania in a large Italian family. Despite the unexpected loss of my mom to heart disease in 2017, I am so lucky to have 3 amazingly supportive sisters, 2 sisters-in-law, a brother, 4-brothers-in-law, and an amazing dad who always told us if we worked hard there was nothing we couldn't accomplish. My siblings come with their beautiful families, 8 nieces, and 7 nephews (for whom I tell myself I'm their "cool" aunt). I attended the Philadelphia College of Pharmacy and Science where I earned a Bachelor of Science in Biology (minor in Biochemistry) in 1999. From there, I went on to do pediatric HIV and DiGeorge syndrome research at the Abramson Research Center, Children's Hospital of Philadelphia from 1999-2001. In 2001, I enrolled in the Philadelphia College of Osteopathic Medicine and graduated with a Master of Science while obtaining my license to practice medicine as a Physician Assistant in 2003. I spent most of my medical career practicing in the field of vascular surgery and have since transitioned to a major global health insurance company conducting medical necessity reviews while providing determinations for a clinical appeals department.

My heart is my 17-year-old daughter Maggie. She was born in 2008 and has not stopped filling my world with love and adventure. We have a shared love of volleyball, Italian language, and all things Disney. I suffered a bit of postpartum depression after she was born. For someone who seemingly had it all together and was completely in control of every aspect of her life...... this tiny baby was now in control of everything. So, I turned to running for therapy and raised money for the Leukemia and Lymphoma society while I trained for my first half marathon in Philadelphia, November 2008. Since that time, I have completed 10 full marathons including New York City, Philadelphia, Chicago, Marine Corp x3, Pittsburgh, Disney x2, and Rome, Italy. The 50th anniversary of the Marine Corp Marathon will be

October of 2025 which is just 2 months shy of my 50th birthday. There might be one last big race in my future.

I was constantly faced with feelings of guilt when school functions were missed. I could not commit to being a homeroom mom due to my unpredictable work schedule. This was the reason I set out to find a position where I could use my medical brain but have more flexibility to be there for the things that mattered in my daughter's life.

While I knew I would miss my patients, my days in the operating room, and coffee breaks with my favorite colleagues, I set out to find a position that was more conducive to the lifestyle I needed. In 2017, I founded Clapperboard Consulting, LLC, which provides medical accuracy consulting to the film, literature, and advertising industries. That same year I also signed up to provide triage editing services to DynaMed, an EBSCO subsidiary. One year later I found myself employed by a major global health insurance company and have been there ever since. We are the first Physician Assistants (and remain the only ones) to be employed by a major health insurance carrier for the purposes of clinical appeals. I am also an adjunct faculty member for West Chester University's Physician Assistant program, and on occasion, I remotely cover the hospitalist service for a University of Pennsylvania-owned suburban hospital.

While I focused on math and science for most of my career, the creative side of my brain has enjoyed painting, exploring museums, and studying wine as I make my way through the ranks of sommelier education and certification.

My daughter Maggie is currently pursuing her dreams as a competitive ballroom dancer. After surviving a shark attack in 2023, followed by recovery and physical therapy, she is back in motion with a Fred Astaire Dance Studio National title under her belt in 2024 and a Pennsylvania State title in 2025. It has been amazing to watch as she transitions from a young girl into a beautiful, fierce, and competitive woman.

It is often hard for me to sit still, so dreaming of starting a company as a working mom myself has given rise to both an incredible friendship and lofty life goals. This book series and its ideas are a collaborative effort with my best friend Adrienne. She and I became fast friends via mutual medical colleagues. Our drive to pursue The Working Mom endeavor developed during many years of friendship, marathon running together, motivation, and jumping the hurdles as working moms ourselves.

While we have chosen to focus our first few books on working moms in healthcare, these books are filled with advice that any working mom can utilize. In the near future, we plan to launch a magazine and host vacation retreats where our "Working Mom" attendees can obtain continuing medical education (CME) credit for various topics that will benefit our own health and the health of the ones we care for in our family and our careers. Topics like "Avoiding Burnout" and "Culinary Medicine" will be offered.

Until we meet in person, Adrienne and I hope you find peace, happiness, and a healthy balance while navigating this lifecycle of being a working mom in any field.

Adrienne's Story

It's hard to believe my working mom journey began nearly 25 years ago. How can I possibly be that old? I have the privilege of being mom to two beautiful young women, and I am so proud of them. My older daughter Danielle is twenty-four. She had an amazing academic career and graduated from Emerson College in 2022. She first put her journalism degree to good use as a television news producer but currently enjoys working in higher education as an event coordinator. My younger daughter Kayla is twenty-two and shares in her sister's academic success. She is a recent graduate of New York University (2024) and will be pursuing a career in photography. They are not only smart and beautiful but also independent and kind, with amazing values. Okay…so how did I manage to raise two incredible humans as a single mom with a busy full-time career? It is a long story but here are the highlights…

First of all, I had help! Thank you Mom and Dad. I had both of my daughters while I was an orthopedic surgery resident. This was not easy, especially since I was the first and only woman in the program. A mere two months after my second daughter was born, my now ex-husband, walked out on us, and if it were not for the help of my parents, and a strong will, I am not sure how I could have made it through the last year of residency (and beyond).

My journey starts with a Haverford College degree. From there I went on to the Medical College of Pennsylvania (now Drexel University School of Medicine), graduating in May of 1998. The following month, I got married and then began my Orthopedic Surgery residency at Allegheny General Hospital in Pittsburgh later that summer. Back then, there were no restrictions on how many hours a week residents could work. This has since been changed to a maximum of 80 hours per week. I was in a small program at a busy trauma center, so we typically worked much more than that and had overnight call every third or fourth night. It was excellent training but also a very demanding schedule.

I first became a mom in 2000. I was just starting my third year of residency (out of five). I was able to take six weeks off, but that was all I could have for that entire year. It was tough, and I struggled a lot with feelings of guilt and missing my daughter. I was beyond fortunate to have my mom make herself available to take care of her. This meant my parents moved to Pittsburgh from New Jersey, where I grew up. There are no words to express my immense gratitude. Two years later my second daughter was born. Unfortunately, two months after that, their father left. I was in my final year of residency with a two-year-old and a two-month-old being faced with the end of my marriage. Once again, had it not been for the support of my parents, I am not sure what I would have done. I only took four weeks off after the birth of my second, and it was an incredibly challenging time in my life. I was determined to finish the program and pursue the career I had been working so hard for, but I was also determined to be a great mom to my two beautiful girls.

Fast forward a bit and I graduated from residency, moved back to the Philadelphia area where I did a one-year Sports Medicine fellowship at Thomas Jefferson University Hospital, and became officially divorced. When we moved back east, we all moved in together and lived as a three-generation household for twenty years. Despite the relative absence of their father, and my work which continued to be very demanding and time consuming, my daughters grew up in a loving home with plenty of support. After fellowship, I took a hospital employed position for 2 years. Following that, I went into private practice. I joined the group I am still with today, almost 19 years later. The schedule after training was not much easier, but I did my best to be available for as many in-school and after school activities as possible. I took as much time off as I could so we could spend quality time together, take trips, and have fun. The day-to-day could be a struggle sometimes, but overall, we made it work. I had to miss things on occasion, but I think that was harder on me than it was on them. My mom could usually be there, or if not, then my dad, or perhaps both.

As an empty nester now, I can reflect on all the phases of being a working mom. In healthcare it can be challenging but also extremely rewarding. Your kids may not truly understand why you are not always there when they are young, but as they get older, they will, and they will learn to appreciate what you do. You will be an example for them of strength and determination. I know my daughters are proud of what I do, and they understand why I needed (and wanted) to work.

As a single mom of adult kids, I realized I needed something to fill the void. I still had a busy career and a nice social life, but I didn't know if this would be enough. In 2018, the year my older daughter graduated from high school, I stumbled upon ballroom dancing. My mom, daughters and I were big fans of the TV show "Dancing with the Stars" and enjoyed going to many of the live performances as well. I decided to give it a try myself at age 46 and ended up finding a true passion in pro-am ballroom dancing. I have now been dancing and competing for 7 years with my amazing instructor. We have a unique, long distance international partnership which is challenging but also so rewarding. I was able to create the next chapter of my life. I am still a mom first, but I know my kids are very capable and independent. They know they can always count on me, but I do not need to count on them… I mean that in a good way. They have been able to leave the nest and soar, knowing their mom will be just fine.

Lisa and I have been on a quest to help our fellow working moms in healthcare navigate this journey since we founded our company in 2020. We are best friends and hard-working moms with lots of stories to tell. We hope you can find value in our experiences. Stay tuned for a series of handbooks which will guide you through all phases of being a working mom in medicine, with strategies, humor, and lots of love and support!

How to use this book:

First: We start with a single question. Based on the answer to this question, you will move forward to the assigned chapter. Simple enough, right?

What is the single most important thing you wish you had; now that you are a working mom in healthcare?

- If you answered, "More Time," go to Chapter 1.

- If you answered, "More Energy," go to Chapter 2.

- If you answered, "More Money," go to Chapter 3.

- If you answered, "More Quality Time with my Spouse or Significant Other," go to Chapter 4.

- If you answered, "More Time at Home with my Family," go to chapter 5.

- If you answered, "Less Stress," go to Chapter 6.

- If you answered, "Better Organization," go to Chapter 7.

- ❖ If you answered, "More Alone Time," go to Chapter 8.

- ❖ If you answered, "Motivation," go to Chapter 9.

- ❖ If you answered, "More Alcohol," Call your therapist and go to Chapter 10.

- ❖ If you answered none of the above, then you are perfect and you should author your own damn book. (LOL)

- ❖ Or alternatively, feel free to just start with Chapter 1 and read until the end. We purposely kept it brief but packed full of useful information.

Second: If you see a QR-code like this....

Use it! We decided to utilize a bit of technology to further enhance this book. Our readers will have access to various cool sites, links to recipes, and strategically placed blogs, as well as other tips and tricks to help you navigate this journey!

Here is a good opener link.... "Unique Challenges we Face as Working Moms in Healthcare"

Lastly: At the end of each chapter, you will find either Adrienne's "Echoes of Experience" or Lisa's "Wisdom from the Journey". We wanted to include a more personal anecdote which may show a success, a failure or just in some way highlight each topic. We hope this will be relatable since we are right there in the trenches with you.

Navigating the Lifecycle of Moms in Healthcare

Table of Contents

Dedication   ii

Lisa's Story   iii

Adrienne's Story   viii

How to Use This Book   xiv

Table of Contents   xviii

Chapter 1: "More Time" .... p. 1

Chapter 2: "More Energy" .... p. 11

Chapter 3: "More Money" .... p. 25

Chapter 4: "More Quality Time with my Spouse or significant Other" .... p. 31

Chapter 5: "More Time at Home with My Family" ... p. 39

Chapter 6: "Less Stress" .... p. 45

Chapter 7: "Better Organization" .... p. 53

Chapter 8: "More Alone Time" .... p. 59

Chapter 9: "Motivation" .... p. 64

Chapter 10: "More Alcohol" .... p. 70

A Letter to our Working Mom Warriors! .... p. 76

Upcoming Titles in our Series .... p. 79

Citations & Contributions .... p. 83

Index of website links throughout the book (QR) ..... p. 84

Lisa & Adrienne

May 3, 2015 (Pittsburgh Marathon)

The day 'The Working Mom, LLC' became destined to happen.

Chapter 1

"More Time"

More time! When we are young, we want the clocks to speed up. When we are older, we want them to slow down. Time is a funny thing. How do we begin to maximize what time we have? As a busy working mom, finding more time in a day can be challenging, but there are strategies to help you manage your time effectively. Here are some practical tips to create more time and maintain balance.

- ❖ **One of the first things to do is make a list of "Needs" and "Wants" for the day:** On one side of the page, list all the necessary things you NEED to do. On the other side of the page, list the things you WANT to do. You might even numerically prioritize the items in order of importance. Start your day by tackling the most important of the NEEDS, then if you have time, move on to the less critical WANTS part of the list. What you are not able to check off on this day, can get moved to the next, always ensuring you are tackling the most important of the tasks first.

- ❖ Use methods like the **Eisenhower Matrix [1] or Pomodoro Techniques [2]:**

- ★ **Eisenhower Matrix:** Categorize tasks into urgent, important, not urgent, and not important. Prioritize accordingly.
- ★ **Pomodoro Technique:** This is a time management method which involves breaking work into intervals called "Pomodoro's". Here are the steps:
  - Choose a task.
  - Set a timer for 25 minutes (one Pomodoro).
  - Work on the task with full concentration.
  - Take a 5-minute break after each Pomodoro.
  - After completing four Pomodoro's, take a longer break of 15-30 minutes.

- ❖ **DO NOT be afraid to ask for help:** We all think we are Wonder Woman, and we can do it all on our own, as if we were stranded on a desert island. This is not the case. We all have friends, family, or co-workers who are typically happy to help. Use this to your benefit. Most likely you would do the same for someone else, unless you are selfish. In that case, read no further. We only want the supportive kind in our circle here.

- ❖ **Pack the lunches and book bags the night before:** It's one less thing to tackle in the morning.

- ❖ **Lay the school/work clothes out the night before:** Do not waiver on this the next day unless there is an unexpected drastic change in the weather.

- **Take showers and baths the night before:** If you are one of those early risers who likes the feel of a shower in the morning, followed by 30 minutes of hair drying and makeup application, then good for you, you will be EXTRA fresh. Unless you are planning to roll around outside in the middle of the night, we guarantee you will still be clean when you wake up in the morning.

- **If possible, get your shopping for the week done 2 days before returning to work/school:** For example, if you work a typical Monday through Friday schedule, get your shopping done on Friday or Saturday so you have Sunday as your buffer day in case unexpected things happen or you just want a day to rest before the new week begins.

- **DO THE TASKS YOU HATE MOST FIRST:** By perseverating over how much you dislike doing it, you are wasting time! Duh!

- **Carpool the kids:** Don't be the sucker who always drives ALL the kids everywhere. Share in this task. It takes a village, right??

- **Prepare quick meals:** This is a no-brainer. There are TONS of recipes out there on the worldwide web for quick and easy meals. Take a peek at our website for some ideas. www.TheWorkingMom.us. Our blog index has a section titled "Lisa's Recipe Corner". If nothing piques your interest there, just use Google or Pinterest, and enter search phrases like: "quick and easy dinner ideas" or "quick dinners kids love".

- ❖ **Practice smart tasking, not multitasking:** Bring work with you to a doctor's appointment or hair appointment. You might as well get something done while you are waiting for an extended period of time to be seen by your medical provider, or while you're sitting there for 30 minutes covering those grays! (wink!)

- **Identify your most efficient time of day:** Most of us are wired to perform better at certain times of the day. There is some research that suggests this is hereditary, having been passed down by our ancestors. If this is true, then Lisa's ancestors were night owls and Adrienne's ancestors were bright-eyed before dawn. If it's possible, try to get the most daunting tasks done during this time of day. You are less likely to become distracted, and you are typically more efficient.

- **Minimize travel:** In a post-COVID time of remote work, many of us can minimize commuting to work. This is a HUGE time saver! If you do commute, consider carpooling or traveling by train so you don't have to focus on the road, and can focus on tasks instead.

- **Don't underestimate the power of a good night's sleep:** Face it, we are experienced single moms working in the medical field, we know how much sleep we need. Picture yourself vacationing in Aruba. Going to bed under the moonlight to the sound of the waves crashing on the shore, opening our eyes to a beautiful sunrise. Getting out of bed when we feel refreshed. That's how much sleep we need. Our body knows how much sleep we need; we just need to listen to it.

Now back to reality. There is work to be done and you need to get up and start your day. Figure out when you must get up to meet that need and count back the number of hours of sleep required for you to be at the top of your game. That's the time you should go to bed. So, if you need to get out of bed at 6 am and you do your best work with 8 hours of sleep, go to bed at 10 pm. Ideally, you'll wake up without the intrusion of your phone or alarm going off.

Additional tips:
- ★ Consistency is more important than quantity. We all get busy, and eight hours of sleep may be nice, but not realistic. Better to get 7 hours every night than 5 one night and 11 the next.
- ★ Go to bed and wake up at the same time night and day. See above
- ★ You can't make up for lost sleep so get up at your normal wake time even if you are up late.
- ★ You can't bank sleep. Sleeping extra to prepare for a tough night doesn't work.
- ★ Quality sleep is always better than lying there with your eyes closed. Alcohol and drugs may help the latter, but they will prevent you from reaching a deep restful sleep.
- ★ Let sleep happen. Don't push it.
- ★ When all else fails. Take that trip to Aruba. [3]

❖ **Time blocking:**
- ★ Allocate specific blocks of time for different activities. For example, setting aside dedicated time for work, family, self-care, and chores.
- ★ Use digital tools or physical planners to organize your schedule.

- ❖ **Delegate and outsource:**
  - ★ Delegate tasks at home and work. Involve family members in household chores and responsibilities.
  - ★ Consider hiring help for tasks like cleaning, grocery shopping, or childcare. Local teenagers are a good resource, as are apps like DoorDash, Instacart, or Amazon.

- ❖ **Batch similar tasks:**
  - ★ Group similar tasks together. For instance, handle all phone calls or emails in one batch.
  - ★ Cooking in bulk and freezing meals can save time during the week.

- ❖ **Plan meals ahead:**
  - ★ Meal planning and prepping can save time during busy weekdays. Prepare meals in advance or use meal delivery services. Marvel at the magic of a crockpot. Endless possibilities abound (Google and Pinterest have thousands of ideas).
  - ★ Opt for quick and nutritious recipes that require minimal cooking time.

- ❖ **Set boundaries:**
  - ★ Establish clear boundaries between work and personal life. Avoid checking work emails during family time. Communicate your availability to colleagues and family members and remember: It's OK to say NO!! Learn to decline non-essential commitments. Saying no is essential for preserving your time and your sanity.

- ❖ **Use technology wisely:**
  - ★ Leverage productivity apps for reminders, task management, and time tracking.
  - ★ Automate repetitive tasks whenever possible.

Scan the above QR code for our favorite workflow app [4]

- ❖ **Self-care and rest:**
  - ★ Prioritize self-care. Take short breaks during the day to recharge.

- ❖ **Limit social media and screen time:**
  - ★ Set boundaries for social media and screen usage. Unplug during family time. Use technology intentionally rather than mindlessly scrolling and be mindful about reducing distractions around you.

- ❖ **Don't be a 'Helicopter' Mom!**
  - ★ Imagine how much time you would save if you weren't hovering over your kids every minute of the day!

Remember, it's okay to ask for help and prioritize your well-being. By implementing these strategies, you can create more time for what truly matters…. and remember to cherish the time you have in the present moment.....

Echoes of Experience

If there were only more hours in the day... I have said that to myself so many times over the years. No matter what, there never will be, so we must figure out how to manage with the 24 we have.

When my kids were young, it was the era of actual paper charts. Electronic medical records were not around yet, so we dictated into a little recording device, and we had a transcription service (those were the days). There were times when it was super busy in the office, and I could not finish all my charts by the end of the workday. I used to carry the charts home and try to finish them in the evening. What I found was, when I got home, those charts would sit on my desk, and I never had time to touch them. I was with my kids until they went to bed, and then I would fall asleep too. So, the charts would go with me back to work the next day, and I would eventually get them done.

Did I need more time for the charts? Yes. Did I want to take that time away from my kids once I got home? No. So, I needed to figure out a better way. When searching for more time, we cannot manufacture hours, but we can create efficiency. I found that if I had some leftover charts, my best bet was to get up a little earlier the next day and finish them once I got to work. Getting up early was never a problem for me, and that was a time when the kids wouldn't miss me, so it made the most sense. Leaving the charts at work, I also never felt guilty for not getting them done at home.

I learned to be more intentional with my time at work and made sure not to get distracted, so I could do my best to finish the charts right away. I was labeled "focused", which I thought may have been code for "b*tchy" since I didn't really engage in much small talk with our staff. Those who truly knew me understood that it really was focus and not the other. It was me making sure I used my time efficiently so I could get the work done and get home. We do what we must, and we should not worry how it is perceived by others.

-Adrienne

Chapter 2

"More Energy"

The Energy Budget: Managing Mental and Physical Bandwidth Like a CFO.

Most guidebooks focus on time management, but what if working moms managed their energy the way a CFO managed financial resources? This concept shifts the focus from hours spent to energy invested, helping moms optimize their daily routines without burnout.

How It Works:

Categorize Energy Like a Budget

- ❖ **Fixed Expenses:** Non-negotiable tasks (work deadlines, childcare, essential self-care). Think of these like basic metabolic functions (breathing, circulating blood, and body temperature regulation).

    - ★ **Work responsibilities:** The energy spent on job-related tasks, whether working from home or commuting to an office.

- ★ **Household chores:** Regular tasks like cooking, cleaning, and laundry.
- ★ **Childcare:** Activities related to caring for children, such as feeding, bathing, and helping with homework.
- ★ **Sleep**: Ensuring adequate rest to support overall health and well-being.
- ★ **Exercise:** Regular physical activity to maintain health and energy levels.
- ★ **Nutrition:** Energy spent on preparing and consuming balanced meals

These activities are considered fixed because they are essential and relatively stable. They form the foundation of daily life and are necessary for maintaining health, productivity, and well-being. Just like fixed expenses in a financial budget, these energy expenditures are predictable and must be accounted for before considering variable or discretionary energy uses. By recognizing and managing these fixed energy expenses, working moms can better allocate their remaining energy to activities that bring joy and fulfillment, while avoiding burnout.

- ❖ **Variable Expenses**: Optional but valuable activities (networking, hobbies, social events).
    - ★ **Family time**: Energy spent on activities with family members, such as outings, game nights, or conversations.
    - ★ **Friends:** Socializing with friends, whether it's a coffee date, phone call, or attending events.
    - ★ **Creative pursuits:** Engaging in hobbies like painting, writing, or crafting.

- ★ **Leisure activities:** Watching movies, reading books, or playing sports.
- ★ **Learning:** Taking courses, attending workshops, or reading industry-related materials.
- ★ **Networking:** Participating in professional events, conferences, or online communities.
- ★ **Meditation and mindfulness:** Practices that help reduce stress and improve focus.

These activities are considered variable because they can fluctuate based on personal preferences, availability, and energy levels. Unlike fixed expenses, variable energy expenses can be adjusted or prioritized differently depending on the day or week.

How will we manage variable energy expenses?

Prioritization: Focus on activities that bring the most joy and fulfillment.

Flexibility: Be open to adjusting plans based on energy levels and other commitments.

Balance: Ensure a mix of activities that recharge and energize, avoiding overcommitment.

By effectively managing variable energy expenses, working moms can optimize their energy investment, leading to a more balanced and satisfying daily routine.

❖ **Debt & Overdraft:** Overcommitting leads to exhaustion—how to recognize and prevent it.

Recognize the Signs:

★ **Physical symptoms:** Persistent tiredness, headaches, and muscle pain.
★ **Emotional symptoms:** Irritability, anxiety, and feeling overwhelmed.

Create a Recovery Plan:

★ **Rest**: Prioritize sleep and relaxation to replenish energy levels.
★ **Self-care:** Engage in activities that promote well-being, such as exercise, healthy eating, and mindfulness practices.
★ **Delegate:** Share responsibilities with family members or seek help from friends and colleagues.

Prevent Future Debt & Overdraft:

★ **Set boundaries:** Learn to say no to additional tasks that may lead to overexertion.
★ **Plan ahead:** Allocate time for rest and recovery in your schedule.
★ **Monitor energy levels:** Regularly assess how you're feeling and adjust your activities accordingly.

By understanding and managing energy debt and overdraft, working moms can maintain a healthier balance, ensuring they have the energy needed for both essential tasks and enjoyable activities.

- ❖ **Savings & Investments:** Energy-boosting habits (exercise, mindfulness, sleep).

Energy Savings

Efficiency Strategies:
- ★ **Streamlining tasks:** Find ways to make daily routines more efficient, such as meal prepping, organizing your workspace, or using time-saving tools.
- ★ **Delegation:** Share responsibilities with family members, friends, or colleagues to reduce your workload.
- ★ **Prioritization:** Focus on high-impact tasks and let go of less important ones.

Avoiding Energy Drains:
- ★ **Minimize multitasking:** Concentrate on one task at a time to improve focus and reduce stress.
- ★ **Set boundaries:** Learn to say no to activities or commitments that drain your energy.
- ★ **Manage stress:** Incorporate stress-reducing practices like meditation, deep breathing, or yoga.

Energy Investments

High-Return Activities:
- ★ **Quality time with family:** Engage in meaningful activities with loved ones that strengthen relationships and bring joy.
- ★ **Professional development:** Invest energy in learning new skills, attending workshops, or networking to advance your career.
- ★ **Personal growth:** Dedicate time to activities that promote self-improvement, such as reading, journaling, or pursuing hobbies.

Energy Boosters:
- ★ **Exercise:** Regular physical activity can increase energy levels and improve overall well-being.
- ★ **Mindfulness practices:** Activities like meditation, deep breathing, or spending time in nature can help recharge your energy.
- ★ **Social connections:** Spend time with friends and family who uplift and support you.

Balancing Savings and Investments

Assess Your Energy Levels:
- ★ Regularly check in with yourself to understand how you're feeling and adjust your activities accordingly.

Create a Balanced Schedule:
★ Allocate time for both energy-saving activities and energy investments to ensure a well-rounded approach.

Monitor and Adjust:
★ Continuously evaluate your energy management strategies and make changes as needed to maintain balance and prevent burnout.

By focusing on energy savings and investments, working moms can optimize their energy use, leading to a more balanced, productive, and fulfilling life.

❖ **Daily Energy Audits:** Instead of tracking hours, track energy levels throughout the day. Identify high-energy vs. low-energy tasks and schedule accordingly.

Daily Energy Audits Purpose:

★ **Assess energy usage:** Understand where your energy is being spent throughout the day.
★ **Identify patterns:** Recognize activities that boost or drain your energy.
★ **Optimize routines:** Make adjustments to improve energy management and prevent burnout.

Steps to Conduct a Daily Energy Audit:

Track Your Activities:
★ Record tasks: Write down all the activities you engage in throughout the day, including work, household chores, childcare, and leisure.
★ Note duration: Include the amount of time spent on each activity.

Evaluate Energy Levels:
★ Rate energy impact: For each activity, rate how it affects your energy on a scale (e.g., 1 to 5, where 1 is very draining and 5 is very energizing).
★ Identify trends: Look for patterns in your energy levels throughout the day.

Reflect on Findings:
★ Analyze results: Determine which activities are consistently draining or boosting your energy.
★ Consider adjustments: Think about changes you can make to reduce energy drains and increase energy boosters.

Implement Changes:
★ Prioritize energizing activities: Allocate more time to tasks that boost your energy.
★ Minimize draining activities: Find ways to streamline or delegate tasks that deplete your energy.

★ Balance your schedule: Ensure a mix of high-energy and low-energy activities to maintain a steady energy flow.

Regular Reviews:
★ Daily check-ins: Conduct brief audits at the end of each day to monitor your energy management.
★ Weekly summaries: Review your audits weekly to identify any recurring issues and make necessary adjustments.

Benefits of Daily Energy Audits:

★ Enhanced awareness: Gain a deeper understanding of how your energy is used and what impacts it.
★ Improved productivity: Optimize your routines to focus on high-impact activities.
★ Reduced burnout: Prevent exhaustion by managing energy more effectively.
★ Greater fulfillment: Align your energy investments with your values and goals, leading to a more satisfying daily life.

By incorporating daily energy audits into your routine, you can make informed decisions about how to manage your energy, ensuring a balanced and productive lifestyle.

❖ **Strategic Energy Allocation:** Learn to delegate tasks that drain energy unnecessarily. Prioritize high-impact activities that align with personal and professional goals.

Identify Priorities:
★ **Essential tasks:** Determine the most critical activities that must be completed each day, such as work responsibilities, childcare, and household chores.
★ **Personal goals:** Identify activities that align with your long-term goals and values, such as professional development or self-care.

Categorize Activities:
★ **High-energy tasks:** Activities that require significant focus and effort, like work projects or intense exercise.
★ **Low-energy tasks:** Routine or relaxing activities that require less effort, such as light household chores or leisure reading.

Plan Your Day:
★ **Energy peaks:** Schedule high-energy tasks during times when you feel most alert and energetic, often in the morning or after a break.
★ **Energy dips:** Allocate low-energy tasks to periods when your energy levels are naturally lower, such as mid-afternoon or late evening.

Balance Energy Use:
★ **Mix activities:** Alternate between high-energy and low-energy tasks to maintain a steady energy flow and prevent burnout.
★ **Include breaks:** Plan regular breaks to recharge and avoid overexertion.

Adjust as Needed:
- **Flexibility:** Be open to adjusting your schedule based on unexpected changes or fluctuations in energy levels.
- **Continuous assessment:** Regularly evaluate your energy allocation and make adjustments to optimize your routine.

Benefits of Strategic Energy Allocation:
- **Enhanced productivity:** By aligning tasks with your energy levels, you can work more efficiently and effectively.
- **Reduced stress:** Balancing high-energy and low-energy activities helps prevent burnout and maintain well-being.
- **Greater fulfillment:** Focusing on activities that align with your values and goals leads to a more satisfying and meaningful daily life.

Example of Strategic Energy Allocation:
- **Morning:**
  - **High-energy tasks:** Work on important projects, attend meetings, or exercise.
  - **Break:** Take a short walk or meditate.
- **Afternoon:**
  - **Low-energy tasks:** Handle routine emails, light household chores, or engage in leisure activities.
  - **Break:** Have a healthy snack or practice deep breathing.

- ★ **Evening:**
  - **High-energy tasks:** Spend quality time with family, work on personal goals, or attend a class.
  - **Low-energy tasks:** Relax with a book, watch a movie, or prepare for the next day.

By strategically allocating your energy, you can optimize your daily routine, ensuring you have the energy needed for both essential tasks and enjoyable activities.

This approach helps working moms optimize their energy, reduce stress, and make intentional choices about where to invest their time.

Wisdom from the Journey

A Moment of Realization

It was a typical Wednesday morning, and I was already feeling the weight of the week. Between juggling work deadlines, managing household chores, and ensuring that my daughter was ready for school, I felt utterly drained and drowning in responsibilities. As I sat at my desk, staring blankly at my computer screen, I realized I had hit a wall. My energy was depleted, and the thought of pushing through the day seemed impossible.

In that moment of exhaustion, I remembered a conversation I had with a friend about the importance of taking breaks. She had mentioned how even a short walk outside could work wonders for her energy levels. Desperate for a change, I decided to give it a try.

I stepped outside with my dog Max and began walking around the block. The fresh air felt great! As I walked, I focused on my surroundings—the chirping birds, the rustling leaves, and the distant hum of traffic. For the first time in months, I felt present and connected to the world around me.

After just ten minutes, I returned home feeling surprisingly refreshed. The fog in my mind had lifted, and I felt a renewed sense of clarity. I sat back down at my desk and tackled my tasks with newfound energy. The breakthrough was simple yet profound: taking a moment to step away and recharge was not a luxury, but a necessity.

From that day forward, I made it a point to incorporate short breaks into my daily routine. Whether it was a quick walk, a few minutes of deep breathing, or simply stepping outside to enjoy the sunshine, these moments of pause became my secret weapon against burnout. I learned that managing my energy was just as important as managing my time, and this realization has transformed the way I approach my busy life.

- Lisa

Chapter 3

"More Money"

We are by no means financial experts, but we know them! Between student loans, childcare costs, and the ever-rising prices of groceries and other essentials, working moms in healthcare quickly learn that saving lives doesn't always allow for saving money. Here are a few tips to get yourself on the right path and/or make a few extra bucks.

One thing the most successful people have in common is having more than one source of income. As a busy working mom, there are several ways you can make extra money without adding too much stress to your already hectic schedule. Here are some side hustle ideas that might work well for you:

- ❖ **Contribute to your 401K if you have one available to you:** ESPECIALLY IF YOUR EMPLOYER MATCHES!!! If your employer matches up to a specific amount, at least do that amount to benefit from their generous additional supplement. It is FREE MONEY! The same holds true if you work for a publicly traded company on the stock market and they give you a discount on shares.

- ❖ **Start a side business:** Think of something you enjoy, then turn it into money! From Tupperware parties (Pampered Chef) to jewelry sales (Chloe & Isabelle, Stella and Dot, Origami Owl…. .etc.), to wine sales (consider becoming an affiliate for profit-sharing wineries), or even creating your own on-line consulting business. What are you good at? Chances are, someone out there will pay for your expertise.

- ❖ **Ask your boss for a raise:** What is the worst that could happen? He or she says no. BUT, if he or she says yes, it is the easiest way you've ever made money, right?

- ❖ **Know your healthcare insurance options: Higher costs do not always equate to better services.**

- **Take on-line surveys:** Take online surveys from your phone whenever you have a few minutes to spare. While the pay may not be substantial, it's an easy way to earn a little extra cash.

- **Pay for access to "VirtualVocation.com":** They list all jobs that can be done from the comfort of your home (hiring everyone including: doctors, lawyers, teachers, web designers, and personal assistants). Working from home cuts travel expenses and car maintenance costs. It's more money in your pocket. It's also a way to claim extra tax deductions for using home office space and supplies. Choose the cheaper monthly subscription versus the yearly one. Then, cancel it immediately to avoid automatic charges. You will still have access to it until your subscription window ends, allowing you a full month to search their database.

- **List your home for rent on VRBO or Airbnb when you are away:** Just do not forget to have a locked closet you can put anything valuable in.

- **Pet sitting/dog walking services:** Many people do not like to board their pets when they travel. It's not far "fetched" to think if they need 3-4 visits per day at $20/visit, this can add up quickly.

- **Sell those clothes, shoes, and accessories in your closet you have not worn in DECADES:** With apps such as Poshmark, eBay, ThredUp, and Facebook Marketplace, there are many places to list your gently used items.

- ❖ **Offer freelance work:** Leverage your existing skills to do freelance work during your free time. Whether it's writing, photography, or managing social media accounts, freelancing offers flexibility and can be done around your busy schedule. Websites like Fiverr and Upwork connect freelancers with clients. You can list your requested rates and availability up front.

- ❖ **Teenage jobs:** If you are starting to get burdened with "wants" from your teens, it may be time for them to start understanding the value of a dollar. It is especially important to explain the difference between "Wants" and "Needs".

- ❖ **Teach English online:** If you're proficient in English, consider teaching it to non-native speakers online. Many platforms allow you to set your own hours and wages.

Remember, the best side hustle for you depends on your interests, lifestyle, and the amount of time you can dedicate. Choose something that aligns with your schedule and feels rewarding while still providing decent earnings. You've got this!

Echoes of Experience

Teach your kids about money as soon as they start to realize how much things cost. Kids will compare themselves to others at younger and younger ages these days. They will wonder why one friend can go on an elaborate vacation for spring break while another can't get the latest iPhone. They will question this even before they truly understand how money is earned, the variations between jobs, whether or not both parents work and all the other factors at play. As they get older, we can better explain that we are doing the best we can, and some families will simply have more than others no matter what.

Our desire as parents, for the most part, is to give our kids all they could possibly want. As working moms, we may also try to compensate for our time away by saying yes more than we should.

I noticed that once my kids understood how much things cost, when we went on one of our many Disney trips, they didn't feel the need or desire to have every souvenir they saw. I had been guilty of needing an extra suitcase on the way home to bring back everything we bought when they were little. As they got older, they understood that the trip itself was the most valuable thing of all.

I think one of the best things we can do is teach our kids about what is truly valuable. I have always been of the mindset that the value of experiences far outweighs the value of material things. When we work as much as we do, it's the quality time spent together when memories are made, and this is truly priceless. High school and college graduation gifts for my girls were trips of their choosing which we took together. All were very memorable experiences!

A quick practical tip as the mom of two college graduates... Start the 529 accounts as soon as you can. If they end up with a scholarship or a less expensive school than anticipated...great, but this is a situation when planning ahead is so helpful. Loans and financial aid can be available as well, but if you are able to start early, you never know how much you can save. Take it from someone who started late. I was very fortunate that my older daughter received a partial scholarship. This was a big help, but I still regretted not starting their 529 accounts sooner. Just make sure you do the research. Each state has its own rules regarding how you must use 529 funding.

- Adrienne

Chapter 4

"More Quality Time with my Spouse or Significant Other"

Balancing a busy life while maintaining intimacy with your significant other can be challenging, but it's essential for a healthy relationship. If you are a healthcare provider who does shift work, it might be helpful for childcare, but it can be especially hard on a relationship if you are two ships passing in the night. Here are some practical tips.

- **You need date nights to maintain your sanity:** Either bribe a friend with a bottle of wine, call a family member, hire a well-known babysitter, or log on to the Care.com app to find a local vetted babysitter. Many parents get so caught up in the day-to-day hustle between work and raising their families, that they forget to continue fostering their own relationships.

- **Get the kids to bed at their AGE-APPROPRIATE time, every single night:** Consistency is key for making sure the kiddoes have enough sleep to optimize their focus and energy for the next day. Once they are asleep, you and your significant other can enjoy the remainder of the evening.

- ❖ Now, we all know that we don't live in a perfect world where EVERY child goes to bed on time every night, but here are a few tricks we have tried over the years.

  - ★ No electronics 1 hour before bedtime. It messes with their brains! There are so many peer-reviewed articles out there that document this.

  - ★ MELATONIN!!!!! You are NOT drugging your kids! As 2 medical providers with over 40+ years of combined evidence-based practice, we can assure you melatonin is safe when cleared by your pediatrician. It DOES NOT make you groggy the next day, as opposed to other sleep-aids such as Benadryl……. SIDE NOTE: BE WARY OF GIVING KIDS BENADRYL FOR SLEEP PURPOSES, AS IT CAN ACTUALLY DO THE OPPOSITE!!!!! Read that sentence again! As with all medications, whether prescription or over- the-counter, <u>ALWAYS</u> check with your pediatrician or family practice provider before administering any new medication to your child.

  - ★ Take a warm bath and add a little lavender essential oil to the water. It's calming!
    - o Wait, are we still talking about the kids?? We need one of those moments!

  - ★ Make a kid-temperature (slightly warm) cup of chamomile or decaffeinated Earl Grey tea and add a touch of honey for sweetening. It's soothing, delicious, and relaxing. Both chamomile and bergamot (in Earl Grey) have calming properties.

Side note: Some providers recommend kids avoid milk or dairy at night due to increased risk of acid reflux.

★ Find an epic book to read a few chapters of each night! It will give them something to look forward to: depending on their age, it could be The Magic Treehouse Series or Harry Potter.

★ Make sure their bedrooms are soft muted colors such as pastel pink, pale yellow, sky blue, ocean blue, muted blue green. These colors create feelings of calm. Do NOT paint their room fire-engine red unless it's a cultural thing or you want to be woken up every night because they are having nightmares.

❖ **Utilize local kid-night events:** Some children's activity centers even host occasional "Drop Your Kid Off" events. They are usually reasonably priced and it's a way to step away and have a quiet dinner together.

❖ **Have lunch dates:** Put them on your shared calendar.

❖ **Run errands together.**

❖ **Buy season tickets to a sporting event, the opera, or ballet.**

❖ **Go to a spa together!**

❖ **Play sports together:** whether it is golf, bowling, bocce ball, tennis, or doubles volleyball, if you are both active and enjoy the same sports, join a league together.

- **Take the same day off work:** It's even better when the kids are in school!

- **Go to a museum together.**

- **Quick check-in's:** Throughout the day, send a text or make a quick call to check in on each other. Share a funny moment, express love, or simply say hello.

- **Unplug during intimate moments:** When you're together, put away distractions like phones and laptops. Be fully present and focus on each other.

- **Delegate household tasks:** Divide household responsibilities with your partner. When both of you contribute, it frees up time for meaningful interactions.

- **Physical affection:** Small gestures matter. Hold hands, hug, kiss, and cuddle. Physical touch strengthens emotional bonds.

- **Surprise each other:** Surprise your partner with little acts of kindness, a heartfelt note, their favorite snack, or plan a surprise outing.

- **Open communication:** Talk about your feelings, desires, and needs. Be honest about what you both want from the relationship.

Remember, it's the small moments that build intimacy. Prioritize your relationships and cherish the time you have together.

- **Movie marathon:** Pick a theme (romantic, comedy, sci-fi, or classics) and binge-watch movies together.

- **Cook together:** Prepare a meal as a team. Try a new recipe or recreate one of your favorites. Put on matching fuzzy socks, light a fire, and make some comfort food.....

- **Wine tasting:** Set up a mini wine tasting at home. Pair it with appropriate foods and explore the world of a wine sommelier.

- **Write love letters to each other.**

- **Learn an unfamiliar dance together.**

- **Learn a new language together:** When the kids are acting up, or you want to escape a boring dinner party, you can communicate in your new secret way!

- **Create a do-it-yourself spa night:** From facial scrubs made of sugar, to oil scented with your own mix of store-bought essential oils, or even pre-made drug-store masks, the ideas can be endless. (Check out Pinterest for more ideas here).

- **Create a picnic, indoors or out.**

- **If the weather is nice, do some star-gazing together:** Try one of these apps, Star Walk or Sky Guide. You can also visualize the International Space Stations. Visit this website for more information: www.spotthestation.nasa.gov

- **Watch your wedding video together or look at pictures of that beautiful day:** Reminiscing of beautiful moments in your life together can bring your bond closer.

- **Build a fort with the living room furniture and blankets:** Remember when you were kids? It's still fun, even as an adult. Bring a bottle of bubbly into the fort and pretend you are someplace other than home. Use your imagination.

- **Virtual travel:** Explore a new country or region together. Plan a trip. Even if you can't take the trip immediately, it is still exciting to research the possibilities.

- **Plan your future:** Dream together, discuss future goals and aspirations. Tripadvisor is the BEST app for exploring and planning.... Also do not forget you can ask your favorite A.I. platform to create you an itinerary for a specific place and a specific number of days. Ask it something like: "Plan a 10-day itinerary in Italy via train, starting in Milan and ending in Naples, with nice accommodation recommendations and must-see tourist sites". You can create an itinerary for anywhere your hearts lead you.

Remember, it's the shared moments that matter most. Choose activities that resonate with both of you and create lasting memories.

Wisdom from the Journey
Moments of Connection

To moms in a relationship, I want to share this: cherish the moments you have with your partner. Make time for each other, even if it's just a few minutes of undivided attention. These moments of connection can be incredibly rejuvenating and help you stay close and supportive despite the challenges of a busy schedule. It isn't just about romance; it's about maintaining connection, support, and partnership even when the shit is hitting the proverbial fan.

I've learned firsthand over the years how easy it is to assume there will always be time later, but "later" can slip away if we don't prioritize the people who stand beside us through it all. So, amidst the busyness, make the effort. Cherish the love that helps hold everything together.

— Lisa

Chapter 5

"More Time at Home with My Family"

Balancing a busy life while nurturing intimacy with your partner and kids is essential.

- ❖ **Look for remote positions:** While most healthcare jobs require a physical presence in the workplace, there are ways to have a career in healthcare and work remotely. Covid did show the world that many positions can be done this way.

  Look for positions at healthcare insurance companies, drug companies, medical writing, and medical consultant firms. They often hire physicians, mid-level providers (such as Physician Assistants and Nurse Practitioners), Physical Therapists, Psychologists, Nurses, Speech Therapists, Occupational Therapists, and Pharmacists. The opportunities are growing by the day due to corporations wanting to save money in overhead costs. You will save even more money not needing day-care, not adding extra wear and tear on your vehicle, and decreasing gas consumption.

❖ **Open your planner and pencil it in:** Make it a consistent part of your week. Do game nights, movie nights, cook together, read together, make TikTok's, and make memories! Even amidst a hectic schedule, set aside intentional moments for your partner and kids. It is not about the quantity of time; it's about the quality. Be present during shared activities whether it is a family meal or bedtime stories.

❖ **There are endless activities you can do at home**: Get creative. Here are some ideas to get you started:

- ★ **Outdoor Movie night:** String up some lights on trees in the back yard, place a blanket and pillows down, and rent, borrow, or buy a screen projector for a backyard movie!

- ★ **Do a home project together:** Take a class at Home Depot or Lowes and bring the project to life at home.

- ★ **Look on Pinterest!!!** Endless ideas there!!

- ★ **Quick Check-Ins:** Throughout the day, send a text or make a quick call to check in on your partner and kids. Share a funny moment or photo.

- ★ **Delegate Household Tasks:** Involve your partner and kids in household responsibilities. When everyone contributes, it frees up time for meaningful interactions.

- ★ **Express Affection:** Small gestures matter. Hug your kids, hold hands with your partner, and share words of love and appreciation.

- ★ **Create Family Traditions:** Establish rituals that everyone looks forward to. It could be a weekly board game night, Sunday brunch, a monthly outing, or a seasonal holiday activity.

- ★ **Go for a Walk or plan a hike:** Explore your neighborhood, a local trail, or a nearby park.

- ★ **Visit the Library:** Discover new books and read together.

- ★ **Tell Jokes:** Share laughter by telling each other new jokes.

- ★ **Enjoy Ice Cream:** Treat yourselves to a sweet ice cream outing.

- ★ **Attend a Sporting Event:** Cheer for your favorite team together.

- ★ **Create Cards for Friends and Family:** Get crafty and spread some love.

- ★ **Explore a New Town:** Visit a nearby town you haven't explored before.

- ★ **Go Camping:** Set up a tent in your backyard or venture to a campsite.

- ★ **Make a Time Capsule:** Collect items that represent your family and bury them for the future.

- ★ **Familiarize yourself with your employee benefits and USE THEM!!!**

Remember, it is the shared moments that matter most. Choose activities that resonate with your family. Create cherished memories and embrace the small moments.

Echoes of Experience

While the pandemic was devastating for the world with significant loss and hardship, I think one positive came out of it for those of us who were able to take a "mandatory pause".

There was never a time since I started residency when I felt like I could truly slow down and take a breath. Then came late March of 2020. My older daughter was a sophomore in college and my younger one was a senior in high school. My older daughter had studied abroad first semester, so I had just moved her back on campus in Boston in January. Six weeks later, I drove back up to Boston to bring her home when her college closed. My younger daughter was about to miss all the 'end of senior year' activities including prom and graduation. Despite the sadness and disappointment, especially for the younger one, this situation gave us TIME together.

I had the chance to have my daughters (ages 19 and 17) at home for 3 months, which would never have happened otherwise. As an orthopedic surgeon, I had a significantly reduced work schedule during that time. We never closed our practice, but we were basically just working half days in the office for those patients who really needed to be seen. We were not able to do elective surgery, so it was only the occasional emergency case, often leaving my OR days completely free. This translated into time at home with my kids, which I never had before. While everyone was scared to some degree and had the feeling of missing out on things, we also had a chance to slow down.

We worked out together, we cooked together, we played games and watched movies. We most certainly felt bored at times and missed our normal lives, but looking back now, I am grateful for the "pause" as it meant an opportunity for our family to have more time together.

My recommendation gained from this is...try to take the occasional, "intentional pause" when you can.

-Adrienne

Chapter 6

"Less Stress"

As a busy working mom, managing stress is crucial for your well-being. Here are some practical tips to help you reduce stress:

- ❖ **Exercise:** Get those endorphins pumping! This is also extremely important. We need exercise to keep our minds and bodies healthy. It reduces feelings of depression and anxiety by releasing those feel-good neurotransmitters, it improves your quality of sleep, and it aids in weight management which in turn will decrease your risk of weight-related illnesses such as diabetes, high-blood pressure, osteoporosis, and chronic fatigue. Exercise also improves memory and brain function in all age groups. Exercise can come in many forms: turn up the tunes and clean your house, join a local recreational sports team, swim, join a gym, dance, or search for free aerobic or strength-training videos on the internet. YouTube is a wonderful resource for this.

- **Mindfulness and meditation:** Embrace mindfulness to reduce stress and fatigue. Practice mindfulness techniques such as deep breathing, meditation, or yoga. These will help reduce stress, improve mental clarity, and enhance overall well-being.

- **Light your favorite scented candle and get lost in a good book.**

- **Listen to music that settles your soul:** This could mean classical for some, reggae for others, and metal for a select few of you iron-pumping phenoms in the gym.

- **Take a long shower:** Use your favorite aromatic soaps to lighten your mood.

- **Have sex:** (Yes! You read that correctly.) It releases endorphins and oxytocin, the "feel-good" hormones that create relaxation and help eliminate depression and anxiety.

- **Laugh more:** There is a reason for that saying, *"Laughter is the best medicine"*. Laughing also releases the same "feel-good" hormones mentioned above.

❖ **Eat healthier:** Good nutrition equates to better brain function, better organ function, and a glowing complexion.

Proper nutrition is crucial to having energy. Aim to eat mostly meals which include natural ingredients. Highly processed foods can cause inflammation.

> ★ **Add power-packed superfoods to your diet:** Incorporate nutrient-dense foods into your meals. Consider options like **spinach, quinoa, chia seeds, and almonds**. These provide sustained energy and support overall health.

- ★ **Consider taking energy-boosting supplements:** Consider researching natural supplements such as nootropics (cognitive enhancers) or adaptogens (like ashwagandha or rhodiola).

- ❖ **Get good sleep:** This will be a reoccurring piece of advice, because it's critical for healthy brain and body functions. There is a lot of research to support the benefits of getting a good night's sleep. As a working mom in healthcare, this may not always be possible, but it is extremely important. Think of it as recharging your battery. If you don't fully charge it, you will not be able to function at your optimal level. Refer to Chapter 1: "Don't underestimate the power of a good night's sleep" (p.5).

- ❖ **Learn to delegate tasks:** We can't do everything ALL the time. Ask for help, get the older kids to do chores, or pay for some assistance (hire a high school or college student as a mother's helper over summer break!)

- ❖ **Make an appointment with a therapist:** This can be done virtually now as well. It's often covered by your health insurance company. Your mental health is critical to maintain. As healthcare workers, we spend an extraordinary amount of time caring for others. We also need to care for ourselves.

- **Schedule time with your best friends:** Sometimes a good meal, a nice glass of wine, and reminiscing about life is all it takes to lighten a mood.

- **Find a "feel good" hobby:** like painting, knitting, or some other creative activity. Pinterest is a great place to look for interesting craft ideas.

- **Plan a vacation:** Even if you don't jet set in the near future, research and discovery allows for a nice place to daydream about for a while.

- **Set realistic expectations:** Understand that you can't do everything perfectly. Set achievable goals and be kind to yourself when things don't go as planned.

- **Create a Support System:** Connect with other moms, friends, or family members. Share your experiences, vent, and seek advice. You're not alone on this journey.

- ❖ **Time Management:** Organize your schedule. Prioritize essential tasks and let go of non-urgent ones. Use tools like calendars or apps to stay organized. Find fast and delicious recipes....

- ❖ **Tap into the resources you have that are a benefit of your career:** As a working mom in healthcare, utilize those connections you have made in your professional circle. Reach out to one of the nutritionists on the hospital floor during rounds and ask what his or her go-to nutritional recommendations are.

- ❖ **Learn to Say No:** It's okay to decline additional commitments. Focus on what truly matters to you and your family.

- ❖ **Practice Gratitude:** Reflect on the positive aspects of your life. Gratitude helps shift your mindset and reduces stress.

Remember, you're doing an incredible job juggling work, family, and personal life. Prioritize self-care, seek support, and celebrate small victories. You've got this!

Wisdom from the Journey

A Moment of Connection

As I rushed to get everything done one morning when my daughter was younger, the stress of the day continued to build. I could feel myself reaching a breaking point.

The final straw came when she spilled juice all over the kitchen floor just as I was about to leave for work. I snapped. I yelled at her, and the look of hurt and confusion on her face made me realize how out of control things had become. This wasn't the kind of mom I wanted to be.

In that moment, I knew something had to change. I took a deep breath, cleaned up the mess, and hugged her, apologizing for my outburst. I decided to take a step back and reassess my priorities. I realized that I had been trying to do everything perfectly, but in the process, I was neglecting my own well-being and the emotional needs of my family.

I sat down with a cup of tea and started making a list of the things that were causing me the most stress. I identified tasks that could be delegated, activities that could be simplified, and moments where I needed to give myself grace. I also made a commitment to carve out time for self-care, whether it was a short walk, a few minutes of meditation, or simply reading a book.

From that day forward, I made a conscious effort to manage my stress more effectively. It doesn't mean I am perfect by any means, but I have become more aware of the things that truly matter. I have learned to prioritize tasks, set realistic expectations, and ask for help when needed. I also make sure to spend quality time with my daughter, focusing on moments of connection rather than perfection.

-Lisa

Chapter 7

"Better Organization"

Discipline and consistency are the foundation for better organization. Without these two qualities, it will be very difficult to maintain your organized world. Start small and build upon it. For example, if you love your morning coffee and have a coffee pot with a timer, make that the consistent thing you do before going to bed each night. Set the coffee pot timer. Before long, it will just be an automatic part of your day.

Next, build upon that task, add a few more consistent tasks every couple of weeks, such as balancing the checkbook, cleaning a particular room in the home, or setting aside a specific amount of time to read, spend with the kids, or exercise.

Side note: If you have a diagnosis of depression or anxiety, it is CRITICAL to develop a consistent plan to follow. Often when uncompleted tasks build up, someone with depression or anxiety can become frozen and afraid of moving in any direction due to overwhelming feelings, which will cause further delay. This can sometimes result in major problems, especially when it comes to paying bills, such as missed mortgage payments, cell phone bills, or credit cards, which can have a negative impact on your credit score.

❖ **Invest in a planner:** A paper one with folders. It doesn't have to be huge, but it should have room to jot notes and multiple activities in a calendar day. Or if you're Gen Z or a Millennial, use your electronic/phone calendar and hope it stays charged for when you need it. Ultimately you need to find the right system that works for you.

❖ **Start your day with a morning routine:** And stick to it! Get up before the kids so you can start your day out on your terms. Having predictable patterns simplifies decision-making and reduces chaos.

> ★ Have your cup of coffee, tea, or lemon water.
> ★ Watch the news.
> ★ Do 15 minutes of yoga or simple stretching.

- **Create a to-do list and prioritize the items:** Separate the "urgent", "important", and "less important" tasks into 3 columns. Use those time management techniques we refer to in Chapter 1.

- **Remove the clutter:** Throw out or sell things you don't need. (If you haven't worn those hot pants in more than 3 years, chances are, you won't wear them again!). Do this regularly. A clutter-free environment promotes mental clarity. Label 3 bins:
  - ★ Keep
  - ★ Donate
  - ★ Trash

- **Break up large tasks:** If the thought of folding all the laundry in one day is overwhelming, break it up into smaller chunks. Fold the towels in the morning, fold the sheets in the afternoon, and fold the clothes in the evening. If you have multiple kids, fold their clothes one kid at a time (or one day at a time if that makes things less overwhelming).

- **Delegate tasks:** Involve your family members in household chores. Delegate age-appropriate responsibilities to lighten your load.

- **Organize your email inbox:**
  - ★ Set up the delivery rules.
  - ★ Deal with email right away
  - ★ Set up a folder and message hierarchy
  - ★ Use 1 email that stays pure to personal messages
  - ★ Use 1 email for potential junk (that you don't have to check all the time). Use it for signing up for subscriptions or online shopping because

these companies can be high risk for selling or sharing your email info. That will lead to flooding of your inbox.

- ❖ **Meal planning:** Plan meals for the week ahead. Create a grocery list and batch-cook when possible. This saves time and ensures healthier eating.

- ❖ **Organizing Your Kids Bedroom:** Keep their bedrooms age-appropriate in decor. It will keep them motivated to straighten it.

- ❖ **Use technology wisely:** Leverage apps for reminders, grocery lists, and task management. Explore tools like Trello, Evernote, or Google Keep.

- ❖ **Centralize information:** Hang up a dry erase calendar. Maintain a family command center with essential information like schedules, emergency contacts, and school details.

- ❖ **Self-care:** Prioritize self-care to recharge. When you are organized and well-rested, you can better manage your responsibilities.

Remember, organizational skills are learned over time. Be patient with yourself, adapt as needed, and find systems that work best for your unique situation.

Wisdom from the Journey

The Forgotten Lunch Wake-Up Call

One fall morning, after oversleeping, I was hurriedly preparing my daughter for school and attempting to leave the house. Amid the disarray, I neglected to pack her lunch. She contacted me from school with disappointment in her voice, stating, "I have nothing to eat and I'm so hungry." The ensuing guilt was overwhelming, and I felt inadequate as a parent in that moment.

We didn't have "DoorDash" in those days. Luckily my mom was able to run through Chick-fil-A and quickly deliver a hug and a smile-generating lunch. I realized in that moment the importance of being organized and making sure I had a system in place to remember important tasks. From that day forward, I started using a checklist to ensure I didn't miss anything, and it has made a world of difference. That moment of scrambling, trying to fix the mistake, and dealing with the fallout made it clear; organization wasn't just about lists, calendars, or controlling chaos, it was about creating space for better work, mental clarity, and efficiency.

— Lisa

Chapter 8

"More Alone Time"

If you like to spend time with yourself, then this is the chapter for you! Adrienne is the expert here. Alone time does not bother her, but Lisa is not a fan. We ALL know it's a healthy thing to be able to self-soothe, be happy in your own space, and blah blah blah (this is Lisa speaking….), but it can be scary especially if you were in a long relationship and then you aren't. But after some work, some encouragement from family and friends, some new projects, and new aspirations, even Lisa is starting to enjoy the freedom of her own space and mind…… (ok, take it away Adrienne…)

As a busy working mom, finding alone time is essential for your well-being. Here are some strategies to create space for yourself without feeling guilty:

- **Schedule "Me" time:** Block out specific time slots in your calendar for self-care. Treat this time as non-negotiable, just like any other commitment. Refer to Chapter 2. This may need to be considered a "Fixed Expense".

- **Delegate tasks:** Don't try to do everything yourself. Delegate household chores and responsibilities to other family members or consider hiring help.

- **Set boundaries:** Communicate your need for alone time with your family. Let them know that it's essential for your mental health and overall happiness.

- **Remember that "Alone doesn't mean lonely".**

- **Practice mindfulness:** Use mindfulness techniques to stay present and reduce guilt. Remind yourself that taking care of yourself benefits everyone around you.

- **Find short breaks:** Even a few minutes of solitude can make a difference. Sneak in moments during lunch breaks, early mornings, or before bedtime.

- **Explore hobbies:** Reconnect with hobbies or interests you enjoy. Whether it is painting, gardening, or playing an instrument, invest time in what brings you joy.

- **Comfort food does not always mean unhealthy....**

- **Virtual socializing:** Connect with friends virtually. Set up video calls or chat sessions to maintain social connections without leaving home.

Remember, being alone is different from being lonely! ***Don't be lonely!!***

Echoes of Experience

Carving out some time to be alone can be challenging when you are in the thick of raising kids while working full time. I have been single from the time my kids were very young, but since we lived in a three-generation household with my parents, there was not much true alone time.

Working in medicine, we take care of people all day and then come home and take care of our families. One way to take care of ourselves could be a little alone time. Once the kids are asleep or if they are self-sufficient with homework, that evening time can be a chance to "steal" even an hour for yourself. I used to retreat to my bedroom, put on my favorite show and just decompress a bit.

It wasn't until I became an empty nester that I realized how to truly appreciate alone time and almost crave it. For some this can be very challenging. While I missed my girls a ton once they were both away at college, I realized that I wasn't lonely. I still have lots of interaction with people at work, I was still living with my parents for a few more years, and I had good friends around me as well. Yet, the time alone was quiet and calm, which for me, was and still is a way to refresh.

I think it can be very helpful as we move through this journey to routinely find a little alone time, even if it's just a couple of hours a week. Enjoy it and slowly but surely prepare yourself for what life will be like once the kids are older and more independent. The more you ease into this reality, the less shocking it will be when the time comes.

—Adrienne

Chapter 9

"Motivation"

Remember why you started out in this profession. It was a calling. Patients are grateful for what you do as a healthcare worker. Also embrace the people you work with. You are all in the same boat and can build each other up. As a career woman, maintaining motivation is essential for sustained success. Here are some strategies to boost your motivation and help you stay on track:

❖ **Set intrinsic goals:** Define goals that resonate with your personal values and passions. When your objectives align with what truly matters to you, motivation comes more naturally.

- ❖ **Embrace learning:** Cultivate an incessant desire to learn. Seek out new knowledge, attend workshops, read industry articles, and stay curious. Learning fuels motivation.

- ❖ **Reward yourself:** Acknowledge your achievements. Celebrate small wins, whether it's completing a project, mastering a skill, or reaching a milestone. Positive reinforcement matters.

- ❖ **Connect with like-minded individuals:** Network with other career-driven women. Share experiences, seek mentorship, and learn from their journeys. A supportive community boosts motivation.

- ❖ **Find the positives:** Starting the day, week, or month with a positive attitude is always a great way to manifest good things. Put on some happy music, keep organized, eat healthy, and drink lots of water. All of these things help support our "feel-good" hormones.

- ❖ **Practice self-compassion:** Forgive yourself for any setbacks or perceived failures. Understand that everyone faces challenges. Treat yourself kindly and keep moving forward.

❖ **Identify burnout sources:** Reflect on where your burnout is coming from. Is it work-related, home-related, or a combination of both? Pinpoint specific stressors so you can address them effectively.

❖ **Remain hopeful and calm**: Do yoga, channel your inner "Zen", and be like a flowing river, adapting but never losing direction. Whatever it is, let yourself breathe, stretch, and find that peaceful space within.

❖ **Request changes at work:** Advocate for yourself. Consider asking for more flexible work arrangements, time off, remote work, or additional support. Remember that it's acceptable to make bigger "asks" when needed.

❖ **Prioritize tasks and focus:** Differentiate between your non-negotiable priorities and tasks that can wait. Focus on what truly matters and let go of non-essential responsibilities.

- ❖ **Adjust your work approach:** Find a work style that empowers you. Whether it's tackling challenging tasks first or breaking them down into smaller steps, choose what energizes you.

Remember, motivation isn't constant, it fluctuates. Find what inspires you, adapt as needed, and keep pushing toward your career goals. You've got this! Being an exhausted working mom can be incredibly challenging, but there are ways to boost your motivation and find renewed energy.

Echoes of Experience

I think a big question for us is how to stay motivated when it feels like you have a million things on your plate, and you can only do them all about half as well as you would like to. This is a feeling we all have much of the time as working moms in healthcare. We want to be the best we can be, but what happens if we feel like we fall short? Do we slide down the slippery slope of saying: "I can't do this" or do we rally and say: "I can do whatever I put my mind to". It can be hard to stay motivated in any aspect of life if we feel we are constantly falling short.

So how can we stay motivated? We must give up on the idea of instant gratification and being great at everything. If your kids are involved in sports, the arts, or other activities, it is important to teach them the importance of practice and perseverance. Perfection may be difficult to achieve, but that's okay. If we teach our kids about the idea of consistency and progress over time, we can do it ourselves too.

I had a couple of rules I stuck to when my kids were growing up and in school which kept me motivated as a mom. I saw over time that these things were important in allowing me to feel connected to them even when I wasn't with them (#1) and in making sure time apart was never more than it had to be (#2). The consistency of my efforts paid off greatly for all of us which kept me motivated to continue.

#1: I always made their lunches for school. I typically did it in the morning. For me, this was the routine that worked. I had to be up super early anyway, so 15 extra minutes to make lunch was no big deal. I typically left for work before they were even awake. The lunches were sitting on the kitchen counter waiting for them, and in that way, I knew they were eating what they wanted, and I was a part of their day. I was always motivated to be up 15 minutes early to do this because it was so important to me and for them.

#2: I would never be away from my kids for more than 3 days at a time. As physicians and other healthcare providers, we must do Continuing Medical Education (CME) yearly. Some of this can be with local courses or online, but often travel to conferences is involved. I was always on the lookout for the quick ones, or if it was longer than 3 days, the kids and my mom would come with me. That was the rule, and I never broke it. This may not really require motivation, but it was something I was consistent with over time which was so important to me.

Motivation + Consistency = Results

-Adrienne

Chapter 10

"More Alcohol"

Ok, if the glass is already in your hand, just enjoy it. If the glass is big enough and holding an entire bottle, then maybe you should consider only drinking a portion of it and saving the rest for another day. As moms, no matter what age our child is, we have ALL been there. We need healthy outlets.

❖ **Review Chapter 6:** Less Stress! Remember that ongoing stress can lead to depression and increased anxiety. If you are having thoughts of self-harm, PLEASE reach out to your doctor or another healthcare provider. They will guide you on the right path to getting help. Therapy alone or therapy with prescription medication can be extremely effective.

- **Everyone takes a time-out:** We must remember that when we (as adults) become overwhelmed, we experience the fight-or-flight response which will trigger one of two responses: shut down or lash out [5]. It takes about 20-30 minutes for this chemical reaction to pass. We have fully developed brains at this point, so imagine when a child's brain (that is not fully developed) becomes overwhelmed. They can experience this phenomenon simply by hearing one word, "No!"

  - ★ We can only get as upset as we let ourselves get. Now, re-read that last sentence. We are the adults here. We need to remember the impact we will have by losing our shit. So, get it together, and if you need 20 minutes and a glass of wine, then by all means, go get it before you say something you might regret later.

- **Remember kids need routines and boundaries:** This makes life less stressful for all.

- **Let go of ALL the guilt you are harboring:** We feel guilty for working too much, not working enough, missing one of our kids' games, missing a field trip. When having asked Adrienne's adult daughters if they felt robbed of her time, they replied "We have amazing memories of all the times you WERE with us. We do not really have memories of when you weren't there."

- **Sometimes food is the answer:** A nice snack can sometimes diffuse a difficult situation. Try making comfort food, whether it's a small plate of fruit, cheese and crackers, tomato soup with grilled cheese, or good old mac-n-cheese. Sometimes hunger can manifest itself as anger. That's why we call it "hangry!"

- **Separate the child from the aggravating trigger:**

    ★ If siblings are arguing, have them go to their rooms.

- **Remember that all kids have different needs:** Kids have different triggers and different responses to your reactions. You may have one kid who simply needs to burn off extra energy outside or they may be the kid who responds to quiet time with a book. Some kids may respond better to a "time-out" chair vs having something taken away. Find whatever works best for your individual child and be CONSISTENT. Don't threaten an action and not follow through because kids are like intuitive little sponges. They will learn that non-compliance can pay off.

- **Learn their language:** Small kids will have trouble with miscommunication and can often act out or misbehave when their basic needs aren't met. Typically, it's one of 4 things: tired, hungry, sick, or if they are still in diapers, it could be a soiled diaper. Do a quick assessment of those 4 things and you should be able to zero in on the cause of the irritation.

  - ★ Note: If your child has impulse control problems, is pulling away from previously enjoyed activities, or appears more tearful or anxious, do not hesitate to reach out to his or her pediatrician or family practice provider. These could all be signs of a developing mental illness.

- **Pick your battles:** If what they want isn't too excessive, let them win that battle. Ask yourself: "In 20 years will this fight matter?" They are trying to gain independence. *"If everything is important, then nothing is."* ~ Patrick Lencioni.

- **Above all, love your children and show them that you both love AND like them:** Sometimes when all hell is breaking loose and they tell you that they hate you, your best comeback can be, "Well, I love you, even though I don't like how you are acting right now." Remember that most kids (and some adults) act out toward the ones they are most comfortable with, because they know those people generally won't abandon them. This is especially true for parents. We will never stop loving our kids, no matter what they do. We may not like or understand some of the choices they make, but we will never stop loving them.

Wisdom from the Journey

The Glass of Wine That Wasn't Enough

It was one of those days when everything seemed to go wrong. My check-engine light came on, my coffee maker broke, and there were 22 cases in my work queue that needed to be reviewed by days end. By the time evening rolled around, the idea of a glass of wine seemed like the perfect escape.

So, there I was, sitting on the couch with a glass of red, hoping it would magically erase the day's chaos, and 5 more cases rolled in. I took a sip, then another, but the stress didn't seem to budge. Instead, I found myself frozen and staring at the glass, contemplating life's mysteries.

I then put the glass down, grabbed my laptop, and decided to tackle the cases right then and there. Instead of stressing out,

I put on some upbeat music, made myself a favorite snack, and tackled them one at a time knowing that I would wake up to an empty queue, and be able to ease into my day with a fresh slate.

By the time I finished the cases, I was in a much better mood. I picked up the glass of wine again, took a sip, and smiled. It wasn't the wine that made the evening better, it was my decision to face the challenge head-on and find joy in the process. Stress management isn't about escape; it's about building resilience.

-Lisa

Dear Supermom,

We see you. We see the late nights, the early mornings, and the endless to-do lists. You are a force of nature, balancing work deadlines, school pickups, and bedtime stories. But amidst the chaos, do not forget to take care of the most important person: You!

Embrace imperfection: You don't have to be flawless. It is okay if the laundry piles up or the dinner is not gourmet. Your love and presence matter more than Pinterest-worthy perfection.

Celebrate small wins: Did you survive that Zoom meeting while your toddler built a Lego tower that crashed onto the hardwood floor? High-five! Every little victory counts. You are doing better than you think.

Have self-compassion: Be gentle with yourself. That inner critic? Tell it to take a break. You are not failing; you're growing stronger.

Lean on your tribe: Reach out to fellow moms. Share stories, laugh, and cry together. You are part of an incredible sisterhood, lift each other up.

Prioritize self-care: Remember the oxygen mask analogy? Put yours on first. Take a bubble bath, read a chapter in a mindless book, or dance to your favorite song. You deserve it.

Rest is not weakness: We know you feel guilty when you collapse into bed, wondering if you have done enough. But rest is not a luxury; it is a necessity. When you recharge, you are not just refueling your body, you're

replenishing your spirit. So, take that bubble bath, read that novel, and have that glass of wine.

Set boundaries: Learn to say no. It is not selfish; it's survival. Guard your time like a dragon guards its treasure.

Visualize your strength: Close your eyes. Imagine a cape billowing behind you. You are unstoppable. Feel that power within.

Breathe: When chaos swirls, pause. Breathe deep. Inhale courage, exhale doubt. You are resilient.

Find joy in chaos: Those messy fingerprints on the walls? They are memories. Embrace the chaos! It is your beautiful life.

Know you are a role model: Your kids are watching. They see your resilience, your work ethic, and your unwavering love. You are teaching them that life isn't about perfection; it's about showing up, even when you're bone tired. And that, my friend, is a powerful legacy.

Know you are enough: Repeat it like a mantra. You are enough as a mom, as a professional, and as a human being, imperfections and all.

Supermom, you are not alone. You are fierce, capable, and loved. Take a moment today, sip that coffee, hug your little ones, and know that you're rocking this journey.

With admiration and virtual high-fives,

Lisa & Adrienne, your fellow mom warriors!

This is NOT the end......in fact, this is just the beginning. This first book is just a small glimpse into a series of books designed to assist our fellow working moms in healthcare on this sometimes-harrowing journey of balancing our careers with raising responsible humans.

So, raise a glass to our Working Mom motto: "Running on Empty, but Never Stops", because sometimes the greatest strength lies not in the fuel that powers us, but the unwavering spirit that refuses to quit!

Our initial series of books will guide readers through the various stages of parenting, from pregnancy to sending their child off to college, with a special focus on those working in healthcare. In addition to these specialized topics, we plan to broaden our scope to include general subjects. Here are some ideas for future books...

A Working Mom Series

The Working Moms Guide to Investing

How To Navigate The Lifecycle of the Working Mom!

By: Adrienne Towsen, MD & Lisa Piliero Drozdowski, PA-C

A Working Mom Series

The Working Moms Guide to Girl Drama

How To Navigate The Lifecycle of the Working Mom!

By: Adrienne Towsen, MD & Lisa Piliero Drozdowski, PA-C

Citations & Contributions

[1] Columbia University School of Professional Studies; Eisenhower Matrix.pdf (columbia.edu) (pp. 1-2)

[2] Pomodoro Technique for Time Management by Beth A. Giesbrecht at University of Nebraska, Omaha (pp. 1-2)

[3] "Don't underestimate the power of a good night's sleep". In collaboration with our friend and colleague, Dr. Jeffrey Christenson, M.D., board certified in Pulmonary, Critical Care, & Sleep Medicine (pp. 5-6).

[4] https://trello.com/home - Atlassian Trello - workflow application (p. 8)

[5] What Happens During Fight-or-Flight Response. (2019, December 9). Cleveland Clinic (p. 71)

Also, a heartfelt thank you to Jeff Christenson and Barry Towsen (aka Dad) for their invaluable run-through and editorial suggestions.

Index of our website links throughout the book.

Intro: "How to use this book"

- ★ Home page link (p. xiii)
- ★ Working Moms in Healthcare-Unique Challenges we Face & How to Tackle Them (p. xiv)

Chapter 1: "More Time"

- ★ The Piliero Family Pasta Fagioli (p. 4)
- ★ Blender Crepes (p. 4)
- ★ Multitasking. Does it Really Work? (p. 4)
- ★ Link to Trello app. Our Favorite workflow Platform (p. 8)
- ★ How Not to be "The Helicopter Mom" (p. 9)
- ★ Cherishing Time (p. 9)

Chapter 2: "More Energy"

- ★ Postpartum Depression and How Running Saved Me (p. 22)

Chapter 3: "More Money"

- ★ Stress During Hard Economic Times (p. 25)
- ★ Navigating Healthcare Insurance Costs (p. 26)
- ★ Teen Jobs (p. 28)
- ★ "Mom": The Uber and Cash Machine (p. 29)

Chapter 4: "More Quality Time with my Spouse or Significant Other"

- ★ Vegetable Bisque (p. 35)
- ★ Vertical Tasting of a Prominent Left Bank Bordeaux (p. 35)
- ★ TripAdvisor Link (p. 37)

Chapter 5: "More Time at Home with my Family"

- ★ Quick and Easy Biscuit Pizza (p. 40)
- ★ Maternity Leave: Know Your Rights! (p. 42)

Chapter 6: "Less Stress"

- ★ Burn Out (p. 45)
- ★ Kids Say the Darnedest Things (p. 47)
- ★ Quick Shrimp Scampi (p. 47)
- ★ The Mighty Chia (p. 48)
- ★ 5 Tips to Avoid Working Mom Guilt (p. 49)
- ★ The Fool Proof Pot Roast (p. 50)
- ★ Managing Stress when you Feel Crushed by It (p. 51)

Chapter 7: "Better Organization"

- ★ Organizing your Workday (p. 54)
- ★ When the Kids Request a Room Makeover (p. 56)
- ★ The Art of Self-Care (p. 57)

Chapter 8: "More Alone Time"

- ★ Alone Does Not Have to Equal Lonely (p. 59)
- ★ Stracciatella Soup (p. 61)
- ★ Strike the Balance (p. 61)
- ★ Adrienne's Advice... Do it your Way (p. 61)

Chapter 9: "Motivation"

- ★ Motivation Monday... Live Your Dream (p. 64)
- ★ Motivation Monday... Find the Positive (p. 65)
- ★ Motivation Monday... Remaining Hopeful during a Hopeless Time (p. 66)
- ★ Motivation Monday... Focus! (p.67)

Chapter 10: "More Alcohol"

- ★ Staying Afloat with Depression (p. 70)
- ★ All Guilt Aside.... (p. 72)
- ★ A Letter to our Kids (p. 74)